The Pioneers of Contemporary China

中国时代先锋人物

樊锦诗

Fan Jinshi

刘小琳　编著

吴爱俊　翻译

SinolinguA

华语教学出版社

First Edition 2021
Second Printing 2021

ISBN 978-7-5138-2104-9

Published by Sinolingua Co., Ltd
24 Baiwanzhuang Street, Beijing 100037, China
Tel: (86) 10-68320585 68997826
Fax: (86) 10-68997826 68326333
http://www.sinolingua.com.cn
E-mail: hyjx@sinolingua.com.cn
Facebook: www.facebook.com/sinolingua
Printed by Beijing Hucais Culture Communication Co., Ltd

Printed in the People's Republic of China

Contents

第一章
敦煌的女儿

在中国西北部的荒漠中，坐落着举世闻名的文化艺术宝库——敦煌莫高窟。莫高窟俗称千佛洞，是中国最大的石窟群。莫高窟始建于公元366年，连续营建10个世纪，于14世纪停止开窟后，在1700多米长的峭壁上存留了洞窟735个，壁画4.5万平方米，泥质彩塑2415尊。这里成为世界上现存规模最大、内容最丰富的佛教艺术地。1961年，莫高窟被中国政府公布为第一批全国重点文物保护单位，1987年被联合国教科文组织世界遗产委员会列入《世界文化遗产名录》。

著名敦煌学者季羡林曾说过："世界上历

史悠久、地域广阔、自成体系、影响深远的文化体系只有四个：中国、印度、希腊、伊斯兰，再没有第五个；而这四个文化体系汇流的地方只有一个，就是中国的敦煌和新疆地区，再没有第二个。”这充分说明了敦煌在世界文化史上的重要地位。

1900 年的敦煌，一个叫王圆箓的道士在打扫莫高窟石窟的积沙时，无意中发现了藏经洞（现编号为莫高窟第 17 窟），封藏于石窟中近 900 年的绢纸书画文献重见天日。

可惜当时中国清政府腐败无能，俄、英、法、日、美等国“探险家”闻风而至，大肆劫掠。中国史学大师陈寅恪曾说：“敦煌者，吾国学术之伤心史也。”敦煌莫高窟藏经洞出土 5 万余件珍贵的文献现在约有 70% 流失海外，保存于 10 多个国家的数十家博物馆中。

1944 年，国立敦煌艺术研究所成立，敦煌终于结束了在民间缺乏有效管理的状态。常书鸿、段文杰等人为了敦煌艺术宝库放弃了优越的生活条件和工作环境，相继来到敦煌，致力于敦煌艺术研究、保护等工作，谱写了一曲曲波澜壮阔的敦煌乐章。千百位敦煌守护人继承发扬着前辈们坚守大漠、甘于奉献、勇于担当、开拓进取的“莫高精神”，其中有一位被誉为“敦煌的女儿”，她就是现年 83 岁的樊锦诗。

第二章

在上海长大的女孩

1938 年 7 月 9 日，一对双胞胎姐妹花出生在北平（今北京）协和医院。她们的父亲名叫樊际麟，毕业于清华大学，是个工程师，先前已经有了一个女儿。樊际麟希望女孩子也要饱读诗书，于是分别以“诗”“书”为名，给这一对双胞胎姐妹取了名字。双胞胎姐姐叫“樊锦书”，妹妹叫“樊锦诗”。当时谁也没有料到，这个叫樊锦诗的女孩未来会在敦煌扎根，并用半个世纪做了一件事——守护世界文化遗产莫高窟。

当时日本已经发动了全面侵华战争，北平已经沦陷。日军接管并垄断了华北的交通、

邮电、钢铁、煤炭、电力和纺织等行业，将华北的粮食、棉花等物资大批运往日本，还强行发行了联银券，导致食品奇缺，物价飞涨。日军同时扶植各种傀儡政权，以达到征服中国的目的。樊际麟不愿意与日军合作，带着全家离开北平，南下上海谋生。

在上海，樊锦诗度过了自己的童年和少女时代。由于是早产儿，她的身体非常虚弱，在小学和中学的课堂上经常因低血糖而昏倒。她还得过脊髓灰质炎（小儿麻痹症），险些丧命。父母疼爱这个身体不好的小女儿，而且父亲的工作也很忙，所以平时对樊锦诗的学习管得比较松，但是她的学习成绩一直很好。

樊锦诗从小就从父亲那里知道，北大是中国最好的大学，北大历史学系是最好的历史学系，北大有最好的教授，于是她高考志愿填报了北京大学历史学系，也没有跟父母商量。

有一次，一直忙于工作的樊际麟突然问起小女儿的学业，樊锦诗说："我已经高中毕业了。"

樊际麟当时非常惊讶："你都高中毕业啦？"

樊锦诗又说："我已经考大学了。"

樊际麟接着问："你考大学啦？那你考的哪所大学？"

樊锦诗回答："我填报了北京大学，但还没发榜，不知道能不能考上。"

毕业于清华、曾经在北大当过两年讲师的樊际麟非常高兴女儿有了自己的选择。

1958年，樊锦诗进入北京大学学习，开启了她人生的新篇章。

第三章
与敦煌结缘

入学不久后分专业，樊锦诗因为小时候喜欢去博物馆看文物展览，又听有的同学说考古学很好玩，可以到处游山玩水，于是她稀里糊涂地就选择了考古专业。

20 世纪 50 年代的北大历史学系云集了当时中国顶尖的历史学家、考古学家。考古专业的师生常常一同外出考察，师生关系十分融洽。北大爱国、进步、民主、科学的传统和勤奋、严谨、求实、创新的学风对樊锦诗逐渐产生了影响，并让她立志要成为对国家有用的人才。

在北大，樊锦诗认识了同学彭金章。两

个年轻人经常一起去图书馆学习，一起去未名湖畔散步，逐渐萌发了爱意，定下了终身。

1962年，樊锦诗大四了。按照北大历史学系考古专业的惯例，毕业班学生需要参加毕业实习。大家都特别想去敦煌实习，樊锦诗也一样，因为莫高窟在大家心目中是中国佛教石窟寺遗迹的典型，是艺术的圣殿。最终樊锦诗和另外三名同学幸运地中选了，她特别高兴。

莫高窟偏居中国的西北边陲，远离敦煌市25公里，地处戈壁沙漠之中。到了敦煌以后，樊锦诗就被莫高窟惊人的美震撼了，“灿烂的阳光照耀在色彩绚丽的壁画和彩塑上，金碧辉煌，闪烁夺目。整个画面像一幅巨大的镶满珠宝玉翠的锦绣展现在我们面前，令人惊心动魄。”

精美绝伦的壁画、宝相庄严的佛像……

樊锦诗一个洞窟一个洞窟看过去，完全沉浸在这美妙的艺术殿堂里。

但是不到三个月，樊锦诗就不得不提前离开了敦煌。原来瘦弱的樊锦诗在那里水土不服，三个月来几乎没好好吃过一顿饭，严重的时候连路都走不了。敦煌的老师怕她出事，就让她提前走了。

“我身体不好，就半途走了，心里也觉得敦煌看够了。因为我过去想来看，终于看到了，我也没想着还会再回来。”樊锦诗后来说。

当时的大学生是国家分配工作的，不像现在的大学生要自己找工作。1963 年樊锦诗从北大毕业后，被分配到敦煌文物研究所工作，而她的男朋友彭金章被分配到武汉大学历史系工作。系里的领导表示，樊锦诗可以先在敦煌工作三四年，然后去武汉工作。

父亲樊际麟知道后，写了一封厚厚的信，要樊锦诗转交给学校领导。樊际麟在信中强调樊锦诗身体一直不好，请求学校不要让她去敦煌，信中满满的都是一个父亲对女儿的担忧。

可樊锦诗没有交。她想，国家需要我们到什么地方去，我们就应该到什么地方去。再说自己已经答应了去敦煌，怎么可以言而无信呢？

樊际麟知道樊锦诗去敦煌的事已成定局后，只对樊锦诗说了一句话：“既然是自己的选择，那就好好干。”

父亲的这句话让樊锦诗彻底长大了：一个人必须对自己的选择无怨无悔。

在北大分别的时候，樊锦诗对男朋友彭金章说：“很快，也就三四年。”

彭金章说：“我等你。”

第四章

磨难重重

莫高窟生活条件十分艰苦，这对之前一直在上海、北京这样的大城市生活的樊锦诗来说是个很大的挑战。

这里的水碱性特别大，喝起来是苦的。喝水的玻璃杯上常常有白印，那是水里结出的碱。吃得最多的菜是“老三片”：土豆片、萝卜片和白菜片。

整个敦煌文物研究所只有一部手摇电话，和外界联络非常困难。用电要自己发，每天只能保证两三个小时的用电，晚上只能用蜡烛或手电照明。半夜里，老鼠经常会掉在枕头上。周围根本没有商店，有了钱也没

有地方可以买到东西。买东西只能去敦煌县城，要走大半天的路。

敦煌的冬天极冷，气温一般在零下20摄氏度左右。平房里没有暖气设备，必须架火炉子。有时候睡到半夜感到冷，起来一看，炉子的火灭了。冻得实在受不了，索性就把所有的衣服都穿上，把能盖的都盖上，再躺下去睡。有时候清早起来要用水，一看水桶里的水都结成冰了。

莫高窟的医疗条件长期比较落后，有病不能得到及时治疗，如果发生紧急情况，连救护车也叫不到。

有一年夏天，樊锦诗从考古工地回来，感到身体很不舒服，就去医务室找医生看看。

医生问樊锦诗："你青霉素过敏吗？"

樊锦诗说："不知道。"

医生于是给樊锦诗做了皮试，半小时之

后并没有过敏反应，医生就放心地给樊锦诗注射了青霉素。注射之后又观察了半小时也没有事，樊锦诗就回宿舍了。

没想到，当天晚上樊锦诗出现了青霉素过敏反应，浑身发冷，还产生了濒死感。她挣扎着叫人，好在医生及时赶到，没有酿成大祸。

樊锦诗后来说："那时候也不是不想走啊！但是常书鸿[①]先生在莫高窟没房子、没电、没水、没交通工具，只有牛车、驴车，他留下来了。段文杰[②]先生赶着驴车进城买东西，夜里回来的路上碰到一只狼，驴吓得

① 常书鸿是中国敦煌学的奠基人之一，首任敦煌研究院院长。因一生致力于敦煌艺术研究保护等工作，被人称作"敦煌的守护神"。

② 段文杰是著名敦煌学家、原敦煌研究院院长、敦煌壁画临摹事业的开创者。独立或合作临摹历代敦煌壁画 380 余幅，面积达 140 多平方米，是临摹敦煌壁画最多的艺术家之一。

不敢前行，僵持了很久，幸好狼没有袭击他们。当时就是这么艰难的情况，他们都留下来了。有前辈在前面，我为什么不能留下呢？”

第五章

牛郎织女

1965 年秋天，彭金章来到敦煌看樊锦诗，这是他们分别两年来第一次见面。樊锦诗陪彭金章走遍了敦煌的每一个洞窟，他们在一起度过了甜蜜的八天。彭金章走的时候，樊锦诗赶到汽车站送他。彭金章拉着樊锦诗的手，只说了一句话："我等着你……"

1967 年 1 月 15 日，樊锦诗和彭金章在武汉大学宿舍举行了简单的婚礼。婚后不久樊锦诗就匆匆赶回了敦煌，两个人开始了两地分居的生活。之后每隔一两年，樊锦诗才能得到 20 天左右的探亲假，到武汉与丈夫团聚。

汽車站

1968 年，樊锦诗怀了她和彭金章的第一个孩子。丈夫远在武汉，她自己怀着身孕孤零零一个人远离家乡，身边没有一个亲人。每到心情烦闷的时候，她就向莫高窟高高的九层楼①的方向走去，在茫茫的戈壁上大哭一场。可是第二天，只要一走进石窟，她就感到再苦再累也是值得的。

1973 年，樊锦诗在武汉生下了二儿子。但她一个人在敦煌实在照顾不过来两个孩子，于是彭金章把孩子接到武汉，既当爹又当妈，把两个男孩拉扯大。

1974 年，樊锦诗光荣地加入了中国共产党。其实樊锦诗在高中时老师、同学就动员过她入党，但她坚持不入，原因是她内心对

---

① 九层楼高 45 米，依山崖而建，位置在莫高窟上寺石窟群的正中，里边供奉的是世界最大的室内盘腿而坐的泥胎弥勒菩萨的造像。

共产党太崇敬了。她一直坚信“共产党员都是特殊材料做成的”，觉得自己根本不够格。而今，她觉得自己可以成为一名真正的共产党员了。

樊锦诗之前曾多次请调到武汉工作，希望与家人团聚，但未得到批准。当时的彭金章已经是武汉大学历史系副主任、考古教研室主任了，武汉大学也不愿意放人。双方单位僵持不下，没办法，最后就让樊锦诗和彭金章商量决定。

而樊锦诗这时已经不想走了。经过了与莫高窟朝朝暮暮的相处，她感觉自己已是长在敦煌这棵大树上的枝条。离开敦煌，就好像自己在精神上被连根砍断，就好像要和大地分离。她想留在敦煌，为敦煌多干点事。但是她对彭金章开不了这个口，她觉得这些年已经让彭金章牺牲太多了。

彭金章知道，自己的妻子离不开敦煌。于是他对樊锦诗说："我们两个人，总有一个要动，那就我走吧。"就这样，彭金章放弃了自己热爱的事业，也放弃了自己亲手创立的武汉大学考古专业，做出了调来敦煌的决定。

樊锦诗非常感动，后来她多次说，如果没有彭金章的成全，就不会有后来的樊锦诗。

当时有人开玩笑说："老彭，人家都是女随男，你倒过来，还是手下。"

彭金章乐呵呵一笑，"我是凭本事吃饭，有什么不好的？"

1986 年，彭金章调到敦煌研究院，这才结束了夫妻俩 19 年来的异地生活。

彭金章放弃了商周考古的教研事业，改行搞了佛教考古。他主持了莫高窟北区石窟 200 多个洞窟的清理发掘工作，并撰写出版了 100 余万字的考古报告——《敦煌莫高窟北区石窟》（3 卷），还主持编写了《莫高窟北区考古论文集》。两个人在学术上比翼双飞，樊锦诗非常欣慰。

第六章

莫高窟旅游预约制

1998年，樊锦诗接受了敦煌研究院院长的任命，这一年她正好60岁，正是退休的年纪，她却重新站在了起跑线上。上任后不久，她就遇到了莫高窟游客数量迅速递增的问题。

莫高窟自1979年正式向社会开放以来，游客人数逐年增加。起初是一年一两万人次，到1998年已增加到每年20万人次。同一时间过量游客参观会使洞窟内温度、湿度迅速蹿升，二氧化碳含量急剧增加，改变洞窟的微环境，极易损害脆弱的壁画和彩塑。与此同时，游客严重超量也影响旅游服务的水平，

降低游客参观体验的质量。樊锦诗想，随着中国经济的发展，可以预计来莫高窟参观的人数还会持续增长。可是我们不能因为旅游开发就牺牲文物本体，也不能因保护文物将游客拒之门外。怎么办呢？

经过长时间的调研，2001 年敦煌研究院达成与美国盖蒂保护研究所开展“莫高窟游客承载量研究”科研项目的合作，对莫高窟的外部环境、文物本体、游客流量等三方面进行监测。

这期间莫高窟在 2005 年首次尝试针对人数较多的旅游团队实行“旅游预约制”。当然这个新办法开始推行得并不顺利，旅行社和游客都很不理解。游客想，我花了钱，想什么时候来就什么时候来，哪里有景点拒绝的道理？很多旅行社也都是根据自己的时间需要安排游客行程的，现在倒过来由景区去调整安排他们的行程，自然会不满意。敦煌市政府也有顾虑，莫高窟在很大程度上拉动了敦煌市的经济发展，现在提出旅游预约制，万一游客不来了怎么办？

但樊锦诗没有退让，她的态度很强硬：必须按预约来！

随着时间的推移，预约制的优势逐渐显现，入洞人数得到了有效控制。游客的总人数不但没有下降，反而有小幅上升。这样一来，大家都服气了。

但作为敦煌研究院院长的樊锦诗明白这不是长久之计，当参观人数达到某一个高度时，预约制起的作用也不会太大了，必须尽快科学地计算出一个洞窟承载能力的最大值和洞窟的最佳承载量。经过十多年的专业监测和数据分析，莫高窟游客承载量的科研终于有了结果，敦煌研究院在2013年正式宣布莫高窟比较安全、合理的游客接待量为每日3000人次。

但这个数字显然无法满足中国旅游热潮下蜂拥而至的游客，敦煌莫高窟数字展示中心就是在游客承载量研究的基础上启动建设的。该中心距莫高窟核心区约15公里，耗资4亿人民币，占地面积约10万平方米，建筑面积1.18万平方米。整座建筑内部包括游客接待大厅、球幕影院、数字影院、贵宾接待厅，以及购物、餐饮、办公、设备用房等。2014年，数字展示中心正式对中外游客开放。

数字展示中心的主要功能是采用数字技术充分展示莫高窟创建的自然、历史、文化背景和不同历史时期重点洞窟的佛教艺术。游客在实地参观莫高窟之前，在这里提前了解莫高窟的背景知识。

现在，游客们先在中心观看介绍敦煌和

莫高窟历史文化背景的主题电影《千年莫高》和展示精美石窟艺术的球幕电影《梦幻佛宫》，然后再去洞窟参观。每个洞窟同时最多进入 25 人，洞内满员时其他游人在洞外安静等候。讲解员配备低音耳麦，以手电筒指引洞内讲解路径，既不损毁壁画又让参观有效、有序。这样一来，游客在莫高窟的停留时间就由之前的 2 小时缩短至 70 分钟左右，而莫高窟最高日接待游客量因此可提高到了 6000 人次。

第七章

推动立法

随着经济和旅游快速发展，国内外来莫高窟旅游的人越来越多。社会上有些人打起了莫高窟的主意，想要在莫高窟保护范围内搞开发建设，在莫高窟核心区建设商业设施，并建议把莫高窟交给企业经营，和旅游公司一起“捆绑上市”。

樊锦诗则对此持有不同意见。她认为，像敦煌莫高窟如此珍贵、如此脆弱的世界文化遗产，对其保护是第一位的，必须有专门的保管机构，不应该和其他景区按一种模式、一个标准进行管理，甚至不受限制地进行旅游开发，更不可将莫高窟的旅游开发管理权

抵押、租赁给企业去经营，“洞子保护不好，我就是千古罪人；有些人要把洞子搞上市，我要是同意，那也是千古罪人……”樊锦诗说。

为了保护莫高窟，樊锦诗把《文物法》和《旅游法》全部研究了一遍，千方百计向上级、向外界反映情况。那段时间，樊锦诗吃不好、睡不好，身体健康也出了问题，但这些困难都没让她停下来。樊锦诗说：“旅游公司懂保护吗？有专业的文物保护力量吗？保护不好，洞窟都没了，还谈什么旅游？”

从决心扭转局面、维持莫高窟保护现行体制的第一天，到事情最后得到圆满解决的那段日子里，她瘦了整整十斤。

樊锦诗意识到，要让莫高窟得到长期保护，仅靠人和技术还不够，必须要有一部专门的法律来保障。于是，她开始思考这部法律的具体内容，并负责组织起草工作。

2003年，由樊锦诗主持制定的《甘肃敦煌莫高窟保护条例》由甘肃省人大审议通过，自2003年3月1日起正式颁布实施。这是甘肃省第一部文化遗址保护专项立法。《条例》坚持了“保护为主、抢救第一、加强管理、合理利用”的文物保护方针，明确了莫高窟的保护对象和保护范围，分清了政府、社会和保护机构的职责，规范了保护机构及其职工的保护、管理与利用的行为。《条例》的颁布保障了敦煌莫高窟的保护、利用与管理等各项工作的顺利开展。

第八章

让敦煌在数字化中永生

随着时间的流逝，莫高窟的很多洞窟及其壁画在逐渐退化和病变。与20世纪初拍摄的照片相比，很多壁画已经损坏模糊了，再往下发展，全都消失了怎么办？千百年后的人们何以领略莫高窟的神韵？这让樊锦诗非常苦恼。

20世纪80年代，樊锦诗去北京出差。一个偶然的机会，她第一次看见有人在使用电脑展示图片。樊锦诗觉得这个东西就像变戏法似的，太有意思了。

樊锦诗忍不住，就问那个在电脑上展示图片的人："那你关机之后，刚才显示的图片

不就没了吗？”

那个人说：“不会！因为转化成了数字图像，它就可以永远保存下去了。”

这句话顿时让樊锦诗兴奋起来，她迫不及待地向那个人请教：“那壁画可不可以数字化保存？”

那个人回答：“没问题。”

樊锦诗眼前一亮，她回到敦煌后，立刻向上级提出了利用计算机技术进行敦煌壁画、彩塑艺术历史信息永久保存的构想。她的构想得到了省科委的支持，省科委下拨给敦煌研究院30万元经费，用于敦煌石窟数字档案建设的研制。于是，敦煌研究院在文物界首先开始了壁画数字化的试验。

樊锦诗想，一定要学习和吸收国际保护管理的先进理念、先进技术、先进经验。于是，她开始在国际范围内寻找合作的对象，通过各种方式、渠道去寻找可以帮助做莫高窟壁画保护的组织和人员。

在樊锦诗的推动下，敦煌研究院与美国梅隆基金会、西北大学合作，成功地开展了敦煌壁画数字化储存关键技术的研究和数字档案储存，开拓了保护和保存敦煌壁画历史信息和全部价值的新途径。目前已经完成敦煌莫高窟 70 多个洞窟的数字化存储，未来将完成敦煌莫高窟全部洞窟的数字化存储。

2016 年，“数字敦煌”资源库上线，向全球共享了 10 个朝代、30 个敦煌石窟的高精度数字图像和虚拟漫游节目。

2017 年，“数字敦煌”资源库英文版上线。敦煌研究院将高精度的文化遗产数字化资源免费公布于众，为敦煌文化的研究者、爱好者提供了方便，同时进一步推动敦煌学研究，唤起更多人对文化遗产的关注。

第九章

让莫高窟“延年益寿”

樊锦诗一方面抓紧建立数字档案，让莫高窟以数字化的方式“永生”，另一方面也在加了对文物本体及其赋存环境的科学保护。

樊锦诗认为，敦煌是世界文化遗产，必须与国际上优秀的文物保护机构合作，将先进的保护理念和技术引入敦煌遗产保护。

1989 年，美国盖蒂保护研究所通过联合国教科文组织，想在中国寻找一处遗产地开展保护合作工作。樊锦诗得到消息后，立即到北京向国家文物局申请，提出在敦煌开展洞窟壁画保护的国际合作。后经国家文物局批准，敦煌研究院与美国盖蒂保护研究所签订了关于开展莫高窟壁画保护的合作协议，拉开了长达30年合作的序幕。

双方合作的第一阶段主要完成了对莫高窟风沙规律的研究，并在莫高窟崖顶安装了高立式尼龙防沙网。防沙网阻隔了从崖顶向窟区移动的沙流，使得每年窟区的积沙明显减少，极大地减缓了对文物的磨蚀。

第二阶段选择敦煌莫高窟第85窟为对象进行研究，希望能解决莫高窟壁画空鼓、起甲、酥碱病害等问题。空鼓是壁画的泥层与洞窟岩体失去粘结，开裂后向外鼓胀，当其无法承受自重时，就有塌毁的可能。起甲是壁画白粉层及其上面的颜料层发生龟裂，时间长了就会脱落，久而久之只剩下壁画的泥层，严重的还会导致壁画消失。酥碱主要表现为壁画整体粉化、酥松、呈糟糠状，最

终彻底脱落，因此它是所有病害中最为严重也最难于治理的病害，又被称之为壁画的癌症。

第 85 窟的修复工作进行了 8 年。光是寻找一种适合的修复材料，中美专家们就用了整整 4 年时间，共试验了 80 多种配方。经过细致的修复，第 85 窟的壁画起死回生。他们还在研究中总结出了一套研究保护病害壁画的科学方法和科学程序。这套程序经过不断完善，已成为中国壁画保护修复工作所必须遵循的规范。

除了不断探索壁画的科学抢救性保护修复技术外，敦煌研究院还在国家文物局的支持下，采用互联网技术建立了莫高窟监测中心，加强了莫高窟预防性保护体系的建设和完善。目前建立的莫高窟监测预警体系不仅能够针对大气湿度及温度、二氧化碳、氮氧化物、风沙天气和降水等大环境实施监测，还能实时监测二氧化碳、相对湿度及温度等洞窟内微环境和文物本体。这就能够从病害发生源头加以防控，努力使洞窟环境保持安全稳定，最大限度地阻止或延缓壁画和彩塑病害的发生乃至最终劣化，做到防患于未然。

第十章
编写敦煌考古报告

20世纪以来，包括敦煌研究院在内的国内外的各“敦煌学”研究主体取得了很多研究成果，仅敦煌研究院研究介绍敦煌石窟的出版物就大约200多种。然而，还没有一部科学、完整、系统的著述敦煌石窟全面资料的出版物。

当年，在樊锦诗离校赴敦煌工作之前，当时的北京大学历史系考古教研室主任、著名考古学家苏秉琦教授把樊锦诗叫到他的住处，对她说：“你去的是敦煌，将来你要编写考古报告，编写敦煌石窟考古报告是非常重要的事情。”著名考古学家、中国佛教考古的开创者宿白教授也曾对樊锦诗说，敦煌石窟的考古报告最主要的目的和意义在于永久地保存敦煌石窟的科学档案，一旦石窟“被破坏了的时候，能够依靠全面详细的记录进行复原。”

樊锦诗一心想做出一卷真正科学、完整、系统的敦煌石窟考古报告，不仅让考古学家点头，也让美术家满意；不仅符合科学性，也要符合审美。但敦煌石窟考古工作的难度和复杂性远远超出了樊锦诗的想象。留存到今天的洞窟，多则1600多年，少则800年，几乎每一个都是内容丰富、辉煌灿烂、各具特色的博物馆。做一部记录洞窟全部遗迹的石窟考古报告是极为复杂的工程，困难可想而知。

2006年，在敦煌工作了40余载的樊锦诗终于完成了敦煌石窟考古报告第一卷初

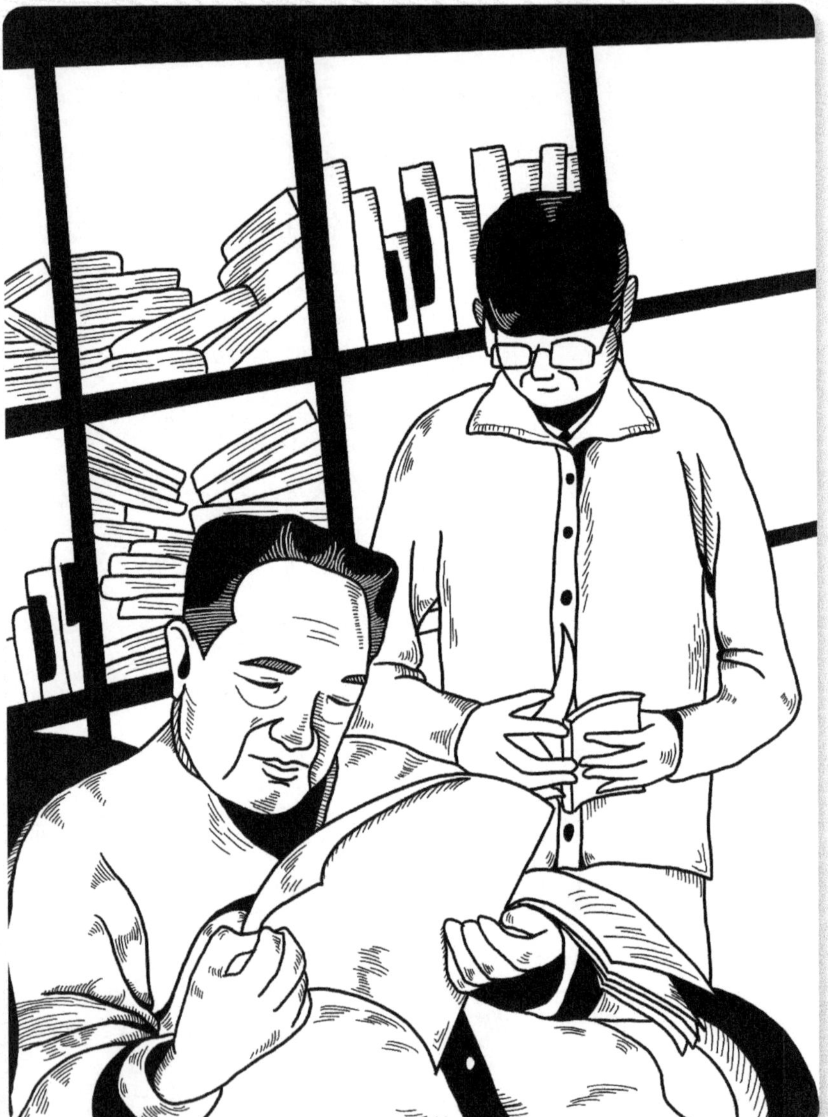

稿。她赶忙送给宿白教授过目，但宿白教授却不满意。樊锦诗遵照宿白先生《敦煌七讲》的“正规记录”方法反复修改，最后年近九十的宿白教授终于说了一句：“嗯，可以出版了。”

2011年，《敦煌石窟全集》第一卷《莫高窟第266-275考古报告》出版。考古报告综合考古、美术、宗教、测量、计算机、摄影、物理、化学等人文和自然学科领域的研究成果和技术，运用文字、测绘、摄影等手段，逐窟记录了洞窟位置、结构、保存状况等，是洞窟最翔实的档案资料。

《敦煌石窟全集》要编多少卷？樊锦诗说，要编100卷！这是一项浩大的工程，需要几代人的努力才能最终完成。樊锦诗希望再编几卷作为范例，后人接手，将会顺利得多。

第十一章
退而不休

2015 年，77 岁的樊锦诗卸任敦煌研究院院长。退休后的樊锦诗仍然在为敦煌四处奔走，继续撰写敦煌考古报告，很多事她还在亲力亲为。

“莫高窟、敦煌研究院就是我的家，已经融为我生命的一部分，人这一辈子能做自己喜欢的事情，还能为它做出一点点事，那么这一辈子就算没有白来这世界上一趟。”樊锦诗说。

2017 年春天，彭金章查出晚期胰腺癌，同年 7 月因病去世。樊锦诗悲痛欲绝，在彭金章去世后瘦了 10 斤。她选择继续留在敦煌工作，她把彭金章最喜欢的一张照片放在身边，好像他从未离开。

鉴于樊锦诗为敦煌做出的卓越贡献，2018 年 12 月 18 日，党中央、国务院授予樊锦诗“改革先锋”称号，颁授改革先锋奖章，并获评“文物有效保护的探索者”。2019 年 9 月 17 日，国家主席习近平签署主席令，授予樊锦诗“文物保护杰出贡献者”国家荣誉称号。

面对成绩和荣誉，樊锦诗一直保持谦虚和清醒。她说：“这荣誉不是给我一个人的，奖章还是和以往一样，留给敦煌研究院。没有敦煌，别人不知道我是谁，所以不要太把自己当回事，要把事情当回事。”

面对金钱，樊锦诗的态度更是大气洒脱。退休时，樊锦诗把公积金账户里存的 45 万元一次性捐掉了，“反正我也不买房了，要

永远在路上
敦煌石窟保管事业的探索和实践
敦煌研究院—樊锦诗
樊锦诗

是不用，捂着这个钱干啥？不是废纸吗？要用在该用的地方”。每次领完奖，她就把奖杯、奖章和奖金悉数交给院里。此外，她每年从自己的工资里拿出一万元，捐给敦煌石窟保护研究基金会，至今已坚持了24年。她说：“只要我还在，慢慢加一点加一点，总能做点事！”

如今的樊锦诗已经83岁了，满头华发的她依然热爱着她的工作，热爱着她的事业。她还在为传播和弘扬敦煌文化四处奔走，不仅到国内外办展览，还主动进学校、进社区去普及和推广敦煌文化。她说：“过去我们要‘进洞’保护，现在我们要‘出洞’弘扬，要让敦煌文化走出国门，走向世界。”

Chapter One

Daughter of Dunhuang

In the desert of northwestern China's Gansu Province lies the world-famous cultural treasure trove: Dunhuang Mogao Grottoes which is also known as the Thousand Buddha Caves. It was first built in 366 AD, and more caves were added throughout the years until the 14th century. There are over 735 caves along the 1,700-meter cliff in which lie some 45,000 square meters of murals and 2,415 colored clay statues. It is considered the largest collection of Buddhist art in the world. In 1961, with the approval of the Chinese government, the Mogao Grottoes was among the first batch of major historical and cultural sites protected at the national level. In 1987, it was included in the UNESCO World Cultural Heritage List.

Ji Xianlin, a renowned scholar noted for his studies of Dunhuang once said, "In the world, there are only four self-contained cultural systems with a long history and vast areas, which exerts far-reaching influence, namely: China, India, Greece, and Islam. But it is in China's Dunhuang and Xinjiang where these four cultural systems converge." This illustrates the importance of Dunhuang in the history of world culture.

In 1900, a Daoist priest named Wang Yuanlu was cleaning the dust in some caves in the Mogao Grottoes, and inadvertently discovered the Buddhist scripture cave (now numbered Cave 17) which had housed calligraphy and paintings for nearly 900 years.

Unfortunately, due to the incompetence and corruption of the then Qing government, the site was plundered by foreign "explorers" from Russia, Britain, France, Japan, the US and other countries after hearing news of the caves. Chinese historian Chen Yinke said, "Chinese scholars all get deeply saddened by what happened at Dunhuang." Over 50,000 precious cultural relics were unearthed here, of which 70 percent were taken from China and housed in dozens of museums in over 10 countries.

The establishment of the Dunhuang Art Institute in 1944 ended years of mismanagement of the Mogao Grottoes. Famous Chinese scholars including Chang Shuhong and Duan Wenjie gave up comfortable living and working conditions elsewhere to come to Dunhuang and devote themselves to the research in and protection of Dunhuang art. About one thousand people have followed in their footsteps, forging out into the desert to take on this responsibility despite various difficulties. One of them is Fan Jinshi, now an 83-year-old woman, who has been known as the daughter of Dunhuang in China.

Chapter Two

A Shanghai Girl

On July 9, 1938, twin girls were born in the Peking Union Medical College Hospital in Peking (present-day Beijing). Their father, Fan Jilin, was an engineer who had graduated from Tsinghua University. Hoping that his daughters would be well read and educated, he gave his twin girls the names *Shi* (meaning poem) and *Shu* (meaning book), their full names being Fan Jinshu (the elder sister) and Fan Jinshi (the younger sister). At that time, no one could have foreseen that Fan Jinshi would later go to settle in Dunhuang and spend half a century protecting a world cultural heritage — the Mogao Grottoes.

At that time, Japan had invaded China, and Peking had fallen. Japan had taken control of many industries in northern China, such as transportation, the post office and telecommunications, steel and iron, coal, electric power and textiles. It shipped back to Japan large quantities of grain, cotton, and other materials and issued paper money to cause food shortages and price hikes. Additionally, the Japanese army established puppet regimes in an attempt to conquer China. Fan Jilin was unwilling to cooperate with Japan in any way, so he took his family and left for Shanghai.

Fan Jinshi spent her childhood in Shanghai. Because she was born premature, she was physically weak and would often faint from low blood sugar levels while at school. She also once contracted polio and nearly died. Because of her fragile condition, her parents often doted on her and they were not strict about her study. Despite this, her academic performance was always very good.

Fan Jinshi knew from her father that Peking

University was the best in China and its History Department was also the best. Since this university had many excellent professors, she applied to the History Department of Peking University without discussing with her parents.

There was one time when her father, who had been terribly busy with his work, asked about her study. She replied, "I have already graduated from high school."

Fan Jilin was surprised. "You graduated from high school?"

Fan Jinshi then said, "In fact, I have already taken the college entrance exam."

He continued to ask, "Really? Which university did you apply to?"

Fan Jinshi answered, "I applied to Peking University,

but the final results of admission haven't been announced. I'm not sure if I'll get in."

Fan Jilin himself had once been a lecturer at Peking University for two years. He was very glad to hear his daughter's choice.

In 1958, Fan Jinshi was enrolled at Peking University, and a new chapter of her life began.

Chapter Three

Meeting Dunhuang

It was during her grade school years that Fan Jinshi first became fond of visiting museums, and she'd even heard from her classmates that archaeology was interesting, and students in this major could travel far and wide. These were some of the reasons why she chose this major.

The Department of History at Peking University during the 1950s was the number one academic center for China's top historians and archaeologists of the time. The relationship between students and teachers was very good, and they would often do fieldwork together. The university was well-known for its patriotism, progressiveness, democracy, science, diligence, passion, down-to-earth approaches and innovation, all of which had a gradual influence on Fan Jinshi to encourage her to make contributions to China.

While at school, Fan met her classmate Peng Jinzhang. Both would study in the library together and often walk along the bank of the Weiming Lake. They gradually fell in love and got married several years later.

In 1962, Fan was in her fourth year. Archaeology majors at the History Department of Peking University were required to complete an internship. All were eager to go to Dunhuang because the Mogao Grottoes were rich with ancient Buddhist art in China. Fan was delighted she'd been selected along with three other students to go there.

The Mogao Grottoes are situated in the Gobi Desert in northwest China, 25 kilometers away from the city of Dunhuang. Upon arriving there, Fan felt amazed at the breathtaking view. The brilliant sunshine on the murals and colored clay statues made them look even more beautiful and dazzling. She'd later described the scene as looking like "a large brocade embroidered with jade and jewelry."

Fan would go from cave to cave, soaking in the gorgeous murals and solemn Buddhas of this wonderful palace of art in the desert.

But after less than three months, the teachers asked her to leave Dunhuang because her frail body was unaccustomed to the local conditions. She hadn't been able to eat a good meal during this period, leaving her very weak and sometimes not even able to walk by herself, and the teachers began to worry about her health.

"Since my health was not good, I had to leave halfway during my internship. But at that time, I felt I had fulfilled my wish of seeing Dunhuang. I never thought I'd go back."

Unlike today's college graduates who go out and find their own jobs, those at that time were assigned jobs by the government. When she graduated in 1963, she was assigned to the Dunhuang Institute of Cultural Relics while her boyfriend Peng Jinzhang was assigned to work in the History Department of Wuhan University. His department dean told him that Fan could work in Dunhuang for three or four years before she was transferred to Wuhan.

Having heard the news, her father wrote a long letter and asked her daughter to give it to the university president. In the letter, he urged the university not to dispatch her to Dunhuang because of her poor health.

But Fan didn't pass on the letter. "I should go where my country needs me," she thought. "Moreover, I have agreed to go. How can I go back on my word?"

Learning that his daughter had decided to go to

Dunhuang, her father only said, "Since you've made your decision, you should do your job well."

These words made a strong impression on her. It made her realize that a person should have no regrets about the choices they make.

As they said goodbye, she told her boyfriend, "Three or four years will fly by."

Peng Jinzhang replied, "I will wait for you."

Chapter Four

Enduring Hardships

The harsh living conditions in Dunhuang posed a big challenge for her. Until now, she had been accustomed to living in cosmopolitan cities like Beijing and Shanghai.

The water in the area had a lot of alkalis, which tasted bitter to drink, and left white marks on glasses. As for food, she often ate "the old three slices": potato, radish, and cabbage slices.

There was only one hand-crank telephone at the institute, so contact with the outside world was a big problem. Also, there were only about two to three hours of electricity every day, and at night there were only candles and flashlights for lighting. During the night, mice would even fall onto the pillows. There were no shops nearby, so there was no place to buy anything. Shopping could only be done by taking the long ride to Dunhuang County.

In winter, Dunhuang was freezing with temperatures dropping to minus 20 degrees Celsius. There was no heating in the bungalows, so she'd have to build a fire in the stove. Sometimes she'd wake up after the fire had gone out during the night. She'd put on all her clothes and cover up with quilts. In the early morning after getting up, she'd see the water in the bucket had turned to ice.

Medical conditions were also poor, so patients couldn't be treated quickly. If an emergency should occur, there was no ambulance available.

It was one summer after returning from the archaeological site, she felt very sick, so she went to the clinic.

The doctor asked her, "Are you allergic to penicillin?"

"I have no idea," she replied.

The doctor did a skin test on her. After half an hour without any allergic reaction, he gave her a shot of penicillin. He watched her for another 30 minutes before allowing her to return to the dormitory.

But that night, she had an allergic reaction. She felt cold all over, and had a sense that she was dying. Luckily, she was able to call out for help and the doctor came at once.

Fan later said, "I thought about leaving once, but then I thought of Chang Shuhong[1] who

① Chang Shuhong, one of China's founders of Dunhuang Studies. He was the first president of Dunhuang Academy of China. He devoted his life to the research and protection of Dunhuang art, so he is called the "Guardian of Dunhuang".

didn't even have a house or electricity or water or transportation, and he only had carts pulled by cows and donkeys. Duan Wenjie[①] even saw a wolf once while he was on a donkey-drawn cart on his way back from the city after shopping one evening. His donkey was scared and did not dare to move, but fortunately, the wolf didn't attack them. Even under such difficult conditions, they stayed, so why couldn't I?"

---

① Duan Wenjie, well-known Dunhuang scholar, and former president of Dunhuang Academy of China. He was the pioneer of copying the murals in Dunhuang. He copies over 380 murals by himself or together with others, which covers over 140 square meters. He is one of the artists who created the largest number of mural copies.

Chapter Five

The Couple Who Had to Live Apart

In the autumn of 1965, Peng Jinzhang came to Dunhuang to visit Fan. It was the first time they'd seen each other after parting over two years ago. They spent eight happy days exploring the Mogao Grottoes together. When departing at the bus station, Peng held her hand and said, "I will wait for you."

On January 15, 1967, Fan and Peng held a simple wedding ceremony in the dormitory of Wuhan University. Afterwards, Fan hurried back to Dunhuang, and they had to live apart again. From then on, Fan could only get 20 days of family leave every one or two years to be reunited with her husband in Wuhan.

In 1968, she had her first son while her husband still worked in Wuhan. She had no relatives around to support her, and she often felt lonely or upset. When she felt this way, she would often walk to the nine-story pavilion[①] in the Mogao Grottoes, crying aloud in the boundless Gobi Desert. But no matter how bad she felt, she always thought her work worthwhile once she entered the caves.

In 1973, she gave birth to another son. As she did not have enough energy to look after two sons, Peng Jinzhang took them back to Wuhan and raised them himself.

In 1974, Fan became a member of the Communist Party of China (CPC). Actually, while still in high school, her teacher and classmates had tried to get

① The nine-story pavilion is 45 meters high and is built along the cliff. It is located in the center of the Mogao Grottoes. The largest indoor Meitreya Bodhisattva sculpture in the world sits inside with legs crossed.

her to join the CPC. But at that time, she didn't feel she was good enough, thinking that Party members were composed of something special, and that she wasn't qualified to be a Party member. But now, she finally felt it was the right time to join the Party.

She asked permission to transfer to Wuhan with the hope of reuniting with her family, but this was not approved. At that time, Peng Jinzhang held the positions of Vice Dean of the History Department of Wuhan University and Director of the Teaching and Research Office of Archeology. Wuhan University didn't want him to leave either. Neither institute would allow them to leave, so Fan Jinshi and Peng Jinzhang had to make a serious decision.

Having worked there for so long, Fan was very attached to Dunhuang and didn't want to leave. She hoped to contribute more to Dunhuang, but she couldn't say this to her husband. She knew that Peng had already made many sacrifices for the family.

Knowing her unwillingness to leave Dunhuang, Peng told his wife, "I will quit my job and follow you," and he gave up his career. He left the Archeology Department of Wuhan University which he had set up, and went to work in Dunhuang.

Fan was very moved. She has since said many times that without Peng's support, she wouldn't have been able to achieve all that she would in her career.

Someone even joked to her husband, "Lao Peng, a woman often follows a man, but you follow a woman and have even become her subordinate."

Peng Jinzhang replied with a smile, "Who is a subordinate? I also work for a living."

In 1986, Peng Jinzhang was assigned to work in the Dunhuang Academy of China. The move finally ended their 19-year-long separation.

Peng Jinzhang switched his research focus from archeology of the Shang (1600-1046 BC) and Zhou (1046-256 BC) dynasties to Buddhism archeology. He presided over the cleaning and excavation of the more than 200 caves in the northern area of the Mogao Grottoes, and published the research report *Caves in the Northern Mogao Grottoes of Dunhuang* (three volumes), a report comprising some one million Chinese characters. He also compiled the *Collection of Archeological Essays on the Northern Mogao Grottoes.* Fan Jinshi was delighted that both of them had made such significant academic accomplishments.

Chapter Six

Implementing a Reservation System for Touring the Mogao Grottoes

In 1998, Fan was appointed President of the Dunhuang Academy of China. By this time she was 60 years old, the normal age of retirement in China. But now she was holding a new position. It wasn't long after she took the position that the surge of visitors to the Mogao Grottoes was becoming a big problem.

After the grottoes opened to the public in 1979, the number of visitors steadily increased from 10,000-20,000 per year to 200,000 per year in 1998. This caused the temperature, humidity, and carbon dioxide levels inside the caves to increase rapidly, which could damage the delicate murals and colored sculptures. At the same time, Fan also worried that the overwhelming number of visitors could impair the tourism experience at the scenic spot. Fan realized that as China's economy continued to develop, she could expect to see more tourists. She was confronted with a puzzle: we cannot sacrifice the preservation of cultural relics just to develop tourism, but we should not turn away tourists just to protect cultural relics. What could be done?

In 2001, the academy launched a research project with the US Getty Conservation Institute on the visitor capacity of the Mogao Grottoes in which they closely monitored three factors: the external environment, cultural relics, and visitor numbers.

In 2005, they tried implementing a reservation system for large tourist groups. In the beginning, this approach did not go smoothly. Tourist agencies and visitors didn't understand why they were denied access to the scenic spot when they paid to visit. The tourist agencies had been accustomed to arranging itineraries for visitors, and they were naturally dissatisfied with the new system. The Dunhuang municipal government also had concerns. Since the Mogao Grottoes had greatly boosted the local economy, the municipal government was worried that the new reservation system would lead to a decline in the number of visitors.

But Fan did not back down, and insisted on implementing the system.

Over time, people could see the advantages of the system, and the number of visitors was brought under control, and even rose a bit. This finally satisfied everyone.

However, Fan Jinshi realized that this approach was not a long-term solution. When the number of visitors reached a certain peak, the reservation system didn't work. The maximum visiting capacity of the caves needed to be calculated. After ten years of monitoring and data analysis, the academy finally announced in 2013 that the safe and reasonable tourist capacity was 3,000 people per day.

But under the ever-rising tourism boom, the scenic spot could not handle the ever-increasing number of visitors. Four hundred million yuan was therefore invested to build a digital exhibition center to meet the demand. Covering an area of about 100,000 square meters, the center is about 15 kilometers away from the grottoes and includes a visitor's hall, dome cinema, VIP reception room, shops, restaurants, offices, and utility rooms. In 2014, the digital center opened to the public.

The main function of the digital exhibition center is to use digital technology to display the natural conditions and historical and cultural background of the Mogao Grottoes and Buddhist art throughout different historical periods. This way, visitors can learn all the background information in advance before visiting the site.

Before visiting the caves, visitors can now watch the film *Millennium Mogao* and the dome movie *Dream Buddha Palace*. The former introduces the culture and history of Dunhuang and the Mogao Grottoes, while the latter displays the gorgeous grotto art.

When visiting, no more than 25 people are allowed to enter a cave at one time. Visitors follow the guides who speak into a microphone headset and lead the way with flashlights. This won't damage the murals and can ensure the visit in an orderly and smooth manner. In this way, the average time spent on visiting the grottoes has been reduced from two hours down to 70 minutes, significantly increasing the maximum tourist visits per day to 6,000.

Chapter Seven

Promoting Legislation

With the rapid development of China's economy and tourism industry, a growing number of visitors from home and abroad continued to come to the grottoes. Some people showed interest in building business facilities in the key area of the Mogao Grottoes, and even suggested that the Mogao Grottoes be operated by enterprises and listed on the stock market.

Fan Jinshi held a different view. She believed that protecting the Mogao Grottoes should be the priority, and that a special agency be set up to protect the scenic spot separately from how other scenic spots were protected. She felt that the management of the tourism resources there should not be allowed into the hands of enterprises. "If the caves are not protected, then I will be blamed," she said. "If I agree to let the grottoes be listed on stock market, then I will be blamed...."

To protect the site, she carefully studied all the relevant laws such as Cultural Relics Law and Tourism Law, and did everything possible to report the situation to her superiors and the outside world. During that period, she did not eat or sleep well, and even fell ill. But these difficulties did not stop her. "Do tourism companies know how to protect relics?" she'd ask. "Do they have relevant professionals and resources? If they don't protect them well and the caves are gone, they will ruin the tourism."

From the time she began this fight to maintain the current protection system of the grottoes until the matter was finally resolved, she lost five kilograms.

She realized that to protect the grottoes for a long time, it was not enough to rely on manpower and technology. A special law was needed to ensure long-term protection. She began thinking about the specific content of such a law, and began organizing the drafting of it ....

The Regulations on the Protection of the Mogao Grottoes in Dunhuang, Gansu Province presided over by Fan Jinshi was examined and approved by the Gansu Provincial People's Congress and made into law on March 1, 2003. These regulations are the first regulations passed by Gansu Province aimed at protecting the cultural relics. They support "protection, restoration, strengthened management, and the proper use of resources" regarding the relics. They also stipulate the target and scope of protection, the responsibilities of government, society and protection agencies, and guidelines regarding the operations of relevant agencies and staff concerning the protection and management of the relics. They guarantee the smooth development of the protection, utilization and management of the Mogao Grottoes.

Chapter Eight

Digitalizing Dunhuang

Over time, many caves and frescoes in the Mogao Grottoes have slowly degraded. Compared with photos taken in the early 20th century, many murals have become blurred. How can future generations appreciate these magnificent artworks if they continue to deteriorate and eventually disappear? Fan Jinshi was very worried about this.

On her trip to Beijing in the 1980s, she came across someone showing pictures on a computer. She felt it was quite interesting and magical.

She couldn't resist asking that person, "Will those images disappear when you turn the computer off?"

The person said, "No, they won't. Once the images

are digitized, they can be kept forever."

These words intrigued her, and she quickly asked, "Can murals be kept in this way?"

He answered, "No problem."

Fan's eyes lit up. Upon returning to Dunhuang, she proposed to her superiors the idea of using computer technology to preserve the images of murals and statues. She won the support from the provincial department of science and technology which allocated 300,000 yuan to the academy for the establishment of a digital archive of the Mogao Grottoes. This was how the Dunhuang Academy began to digitize the murals.

Fan focused on learning the advanced concepts, technology, and managerial expertise from international protection agencies. She began to seek partners across the world to cooperate with her in protecting the murals of the Mogao Grottoes.

Promoted by her, the Dunhuang Academy began cooperating with the USA's Mellon Foundation and also Northwestern University to carry out the research in key technologies used in the digital archiving and storage of historical information of the Dunhuang murals. At present, the digital archiving of over 70 grottoes has been completed, with all the grottoes in Dunhuang to be completed in the future.

In 2016, the "Digital Dunhuang" resource library was launched, consisting of virtual travel programs and high-definition images of 30 Dunhuang grottoes across 10 dynasties, to be available online to anyone in the world.

In 2017, the English version was launched so that scholars and those interested in Dunhuang culture can easily get access to the cultural heritage resources. This can further promote the studies of Dunhuang and draw greater attention to its cultural heritage.

Chapter Nine

Prolonging the Life of the Mogao Grottoes

Fan Jinshi stepped up efforts to establish the digital archive so that the Mogao Grottoes could be "immortalized" in a digital way. In addition to this, she has done a lot to strengthen the protection of the cultural relics and their surroundings.

As the grottoes are a part of the world's cultural heritage, she believes it is necessary to cooperate with outstanding international cultural relics protection agencies to introduce advanced concepts and technology from abroad to strengthen the protection of the Dunhuang relics.

In 1989, the US Getty Conservation Institute, through UNESCO, was seeking a heritage site in China to carry out conservation cooperation work.

Upon hearing the news, Fan immediately went to the National Cultural Heritage Administration of China in Beijing to apply for the international cooperation project with the aim of protecting the frescoes of Dunhuang. Through the approval of the administration, the Dunhuang Academy signed the cooperation project with the Getty Conservation Institute, ushering in a 30-year cooperation project.

The first phase of the project involved researching sand and wind patterns of the Mogao Grottoes. They installed nylon sand-resistant nets on top of the grottoes to prevent sand from entering the caves, thereby reducing annual sand accumulation, which would greatly slow the erosion of the relics.

The second phase focused on Cave 85, and how to resolve the problem of swollen and peeling frescoes and the imbalance between acid and alkali. The swollen frescoes are often caused by the splits between the rock layer and the outer painting layer.

When the outer layer came off, the murals were likely to cave in. Peeling frescoes are those whose paint has begun to come off. As time goes by, the murals will disappear, and all that will remain is the clay layer beneath. The imbalance between acid and alkali may lead to the softening or even disappearance of the mural paint as it becomes powdered and loose and falls off. This is the most severe problem, also known as the "cancer" of murals.

Chinese and American experts spent four years finding the best material for restoration from over 80 options. It took them altogether eight years to restore the wall paintings in Cave 85. During their research, they developed some approaches to protect the eroding murals. The improved approaches have now become the standards for protecting and restoring Chinese murals.

With the support of the National Cultural Heritage Administration, the Dunhuang Academy established the Mogao Grottoes Monitoring Center which uses internet technology to strengthen early warning protection system. The center can monitor not only external environmental factors such as temperature, humidity, carbon dioxide, nitrogen oxide, wind, sand, weather and precipitation, but also the internal cave environment factors like carbon dioxide, relative humidity, and temperature. In this way, damage and erosion can be prevented by minimizing the negative effects of these factors on the murals and statues.

Chapter Ten

Writing the Archeological Report on Dunhuang

There has been much domestic and international research in the 20th century on the Mogao Grottoes, and the Dunhuang Academy alone has released over 200 publications on the subject. However, there has been no comprehensive book with a scientific and systematic introduction to the Mogao Grottoes.

Before Fan left for Dunhuang to work, Professor Su Bingqi, famous archaeologist and Dean of the Archeology Department of Peking University, invited Fan to his home. He told her, "When you work in Dunhuang, you'll surely write some reports on the Dunhuang Mogao Grottoes. This job is very important."

Professor Su Bai, a pioneer of Buddhist archeology, also told her, "The main purpose of these reports is to preserve the Mogao Grottoes forever. If any damage occurred to the caves, we would still have detailed records to restore them."

Fan wanted to write a comprehensive and systematic report on the Mogao Grottoes which could satisfy everyone in both the scientific and aesthetic communities. She had never imagined, however, that the archeological work would be so complicated. The earliest works in the caves date back some 1,600 years, with the latest works dating back some 800 years, encompassing many different dynasties and cultures. Each cave could be considered its own museum due to the rich and unique content inside. Writing a thorough, archeological report on all the caves, therefore, was an extremely complicated project.

In 2006, after working 40 years on the project, Fan

finally completed the first draft of the first volume of the "Mogao Grottoes Archaeological Report". She sent the draft to Professor Su Bai for a review, but he was not satisfied. She revised it over and over again based on the approaches introduced by Professor Su in his book *Seven Lectures on Dunhuang*. Finally, at almost 90 years old, Professor Su sent her a reply: "OK, now you can publish it."

In 2011, the first volume of *Complete Collection of Dunhuang Grottoes (Caves 266-275)* was published. The report incorporates the research results of such disciplines as archeology, fine arts, religion, surveying, IT, photography, physics, chemistry, etc., and records the positions, structures, and conservation of the caves in scripts and images. It is one of the most detailed reports ever published on the conditions of the grottoes.

How many volumes should be compiled? "One hundred," said Fan Jinshi. She said it was a huge project which would require the efforts of several generations to complete. She hoped to compile several more volumes to serve as examples for later generations to ensure the process continues smoothly.

Chapter Eleven

Keeping Working after Retirement

In 2015, the 77-year-old Fan Jinshi retired from her post as the President of the Dunhuang Academy. But this did not stop her. She has continued to write reports and conduct her own research.

"The Mogao Grottoes and the Dunhuang Academy are my family; they are part of my life," she has said. "I feel my life has been very rewarding because I've been doing what I love and have been contributing my small part."

In the spring of 2017, Peng Jinzhang was diagnosed with advanced pancreatic cancer and died in July that year. After his death, Fan was so distraught that she lost some five kilograms. However, she chose to stay and work in Dunhuang, and kept a favorite photo of Peng by her side, as if he'd never left.

On December 18, 2018, the CPC Central Committee and the State Council recognized Fan Jinshi's work and awarded her the titles of "Reform Pioneer", "Explorer of Effective Protection of Cultural Relics", and the Reform Pioneer Medal. On September 17, 2019, President Xi Jinping signed a presidential order giving her the national honorary title "Outstanding Contributor to Cultural Relics Protection".

Upon receiving these honors, Fan Jinshi has remained humble, saying, "These honors don't belong to me. I will give my medals to the academy. Without Dunhuang, no one would have heard of me. Don't ever take yourself too seriously, but instead take what you do very seriously."

Fan has also been very generous with money. When she retired, she donated 450,000 yuan from her housing provident fund to the academy, saying

"I'm not going to buy a house, so it's useless for me to keep this money. It should be spent where it is most needed." Every time she has received a prize, she has handed over the money, trophies and medals to the academy. Also, she has been donating 10,000 yuan per year from her salary to the Mogao Grottoes Preservation and Research Foundation. She has been doing this for the past 24 years. "As long as I live," she has said, "I can add a little bit here and there and can always do something!"

Now 83 years old and gray-haired, Fan Jinshi still loves her cause. She still travels here and there, promoting Dunhuang culture. She hosts exhibitions at home and abroad, and goes to schools and communities to promote Dunhuang culture. She has said, "In the past, we wandered into caves to protect cultural relics there, but now we are exiting the caves to promote them. We need to do more to go out and tell people in the world about Dunhuang culture."

出版策划：王君校　韩　晖
统筹协调：付　眉　韩　颖　彭　博
责任编辑：张　杨　翟淑蓉
英文编辑：吴爱俊
封面设计：智玖拾（成都）文化传媒有限公司
印刷监制：汪　洋

图书在版编目（CIP）数据

樊锦诗：汉英对照 / 刘小琳编著；吴爱俊翻译 .-- 北京：华语教学出版社，2021.6
（中国时代先锋人物）
ISBN 978-7-5138-2104-9

Ⅰ. ①樊… Ⅱ. ①刘… ②吴… Ⅲ. ①樊锦诗－生平事迹 Ⅳ. ① D263

中国版本图书馆 CIP 数据核字（2021）第 051946 号

樊锦诗
刘小琳　编著
吴爱俊　翻译
*

华语教学出版社有限责任公司出版
（中国北京百万庄大街 24 号　邮政编码 100037）
电话：(86)10-68320585, 68997826
传真：(86)10-68997826, 68326333
网址：www.sinolingua.com.cn
电子信箱：hyjx@sinolingua.com.cn
北京虎彩文化传播有限公司印刷
2021 年（32 开）第 1 版
2021 年第 1 版第 2 次印刷
ISBN 978-7-5138-2104-9
003990